A Fishy Business

A One Act Play

by Margaret Wood

WWW.SAMUELFRENCH.CO.UK
WWW.SAMUELFRENCH.COM

FOR AMATEUR PRODUCTION ENQUIRIES

UNITED KINGDOM AND WORLD EXCLUDING NORTH AMERICA

plays@SamuelFrench-London.co.uk

020 7255 4302/01

Each title is subject to availability from Samuel French,

depending upon country of performance.

CHARACTERS

MARY	
GEORGE	her husband
THE VICAR	
MRS MASTERS	his wife
EMMELINE WAGSTAFFE	a friend
UNCLE RICHARD	
NIGEL	George and Mary's son
FELICITY	his girlfriend
TWO AMBULANCE MEN	virtually extras

SCENE: The sitting room of George and Mary's house.

TIME: Evening.

There is an acting fee of £1.75 on each and every performance of A FISHY BUSINESS. The fee is payable to Evans Brothers Limited, Montague House, Russell Square, London WC1B 5BX or any of their authorised agents overseas, who will then issue a licence giving permission for the performance to take place. A licence MUST be issued before any representation may take place. The fee cannot in any circumstances be varied or waived.

AGENTS

from whom copies and licences may be obtained

AUSTRALIA	Will Andrade, 275c Pitt Street, Sydney.
NEW ZEALAND	The Play Bureau, Box 3611, Wellington.
SOUTH AFRICA	Darters, P.O. Box 174, Cape Town.
RHODESIA	A.R.T.S., P.O. Box 2701, Salisbury.
KENYA	Theatrical Enterprises (Kenya) Ltd., P.O.Box 30333 Nairobi.

ISBN 0 237 74980 7

Printed in Great Britain by Lewis Reprints Ltd., member of Brown Knight & Truscott Group London and Tonbridge

A FISHY BUSINESS

The sitting room of GEORGE and MARY's house. It is comfortably and conventionally furnished. U.C., an alcove, with a rostrum in it to give the effect of leading to another room, with the dining room supposed off L. U.R. there is an exit to the hall and another D.L. to the kitchen.

GEORGE is sitting by the fireplace R. behind a newspaper from which he emerges only momentarily at long intervals. He is in his shirt sleeves and has obviously been gardening. After a few seconds pause, MARY's voice is heard calling from the kitchen, L.

MARY	(off) George.
	(GEORGE takes no notice.)
	George! Are you dressed? (Pause.) George!
GEORGE	Um?
MARY	Are you dressed?
GEORGE	(absently) Yes.
MARY	Good. Because they'll be here in a few minutes. (Change of tone to fond wheedling.) Hallo, my sweetie-pie. Where you been, then? Is you hungry, Tiddly winks? Never mind. Mummy will get you something in a minute.

GEORGE   (lowering paper and looking L.)   Bloody cat!
              (He gives the paper a shake and returns to it.)

MARY   (entering with large plate and crossing to dining room)
              Mummy's just got to finish off the table and then Tiddles
              shall have a lovely saucer of milky-wilky.

GEORGE   (joining in savagely)   Saucer of milky-wilky.

MARY   (off)   Oh, it does look lovely. Come and look,
              darling. Fresh salmon gives such tone to a table.

              (GEORGE goes on reading.)

              George!

GEORGE   Um?

MARY   Didn't you hear me?   (She comes to alcove C.)
              I said, come and look.

GEORGE   Me? You said 'darling'.

MARY   Well?

GEORGE   Naturally, I thought you meant that damned cat.

MARY   (coming forward)   There's no need to be offensive,
              George.   (Sees his clothes.)   George! You
              liar.

GEORGE   That's more like it. Now I know where I am.

MARY   You said you were dressed.

GEORGE   Well? Am I in the nude?

MARY   Don't be cheap. You deliberately prevaricated.

GEORGE   There's words.

MARY   Go up and change at once. They'll be here in ten
              minutes.

GEORGE   It takes me five to change. I don't have to do my face
              over and put on my hair piece.   (He continues to
              study his paper.)

MARY   Typical. I spend most of the day slaving over the
              supper –

GEORGE   To the exclusion of lunch –

MARY   I invite the right people, I try, in spite of your
            persistent non-co-operation to help you up the social
            ladder -

GEORGE   The adverts say you need only a tin of peas to do that -

MARY   You're crude, George. Gracious living is wasted on
            you. Fresh salmon - a whole fresh salmon caught by
            Uncle Richard and you talk about tinned peas. I'd have
            you know that not a tin-opener has been used in this
            house today.

GEORGE   Makes a change.

MARY   (dissolving into angry tears)   It means nothing to
            you, nothing, that I'm worn out. I haven't sat down
            except for a snack -

GEORGE   Corned beef. Come to think of it - that was tinned.

MARY   (snapping)   Opened yesterday.

GEORGE   Okay. You win on points. Dry those tears; there's too
            much vinegar in the salad already.   (Looks at
            watch.)   The time lag is now reduced to five
            minutes. I shall go and change.   (He heaves
            himself up, dropping the paper on the floor. Leaving
            his shoes behind, he departs in stockinged feet.)

MARY   (picking up shoes)   Take your shoes with you.
            (Sniffs.)   And I should change your socks if I were
            you.

GEORGE   (taking shoes and going)   Clean on yesterday.
            (He exits to hall.)

MARY   A day too long.   (She picks up the papers in
            exasperation.)   Just a donkey on a treadmill.
            Round and round till you drop.

GEORGE   (off)   Mary, where's the blue shirt?

MARY   In the wash. It's too casual, anyway. I put out the
            white one.   (She moves round the room, plumping
            up cushions etc., muttering in martyrdom.)   Pick
            up, clean up, wash up, break down. That's a woman's
            life.

GEORGE   (off)   White shirt won't do.

MARY   It will!

GEORGE   (entering in shirt with cuffs hanging over his
                  outstretched wrists)   No button on cuff.   (Look
                  at other sleeve.)   No button on both cuffs.

MARY   (stamping)   If only you'd got ready earlier. I told
                  you. I can't sew buttons on now. I've got all the last
                  minute things to do.

GEORGE   (going)   Not to worry, not to worry. I can turn up
                  the cuffs so that they don't show.

MARY   But they ought to show. You've got such knobbly
                  wrists.   (She moves into dining room.)   I'll do
                  them if I have time. Maybe they'll all be late and
                  then I can -   (There is a moment's silence and then
                  a piercing shriek. She returns wildly.)   George!
                  George!   (She carries the large plate.)

GEORGE   (rushing in, trousers in hand)   What the hell now?

MARY   The salmon! Our beautiful salmon -

GEORGE   What about it?

MARY   The cat - the cat got at it. He must have got through
                  the window.

GEORGE   (regarding dish)   Looks as if it's been bombed out.

MARY   (sinking into chair and regarding the dish dolefully)
                  Ruined. What on earth shall I do? And Uncle Richard
                  coming.

GEORGE   Where's that bloody Tiddly-Winks?   (He creeps
                  towards the dining room, calling sweetly.)
                  Tiddly-widdly puss, puss, puss. Where are you, then?
                  Come to Daddy, honest katkin. Nothing to be scared
                  of.   (Suddenly charges into dining room.)
                  A-ah! Got you, you thieving, ungrateful, little swine
                  Grrh! Get out of it.   (If feasible, he can cross
                  down to kitchen carrying an actual cat by the scruff
                  of the neck. If not, there can be a bang from the
                  dining room as if he has thrown it out from there. He
                  returns.)   And may he lose all his nine twisted,

	little lives. (He looks at the plate.) Clean out of the middle. The unkindest cut of all.
MARY	(wailing) What'll I do, what'll I do? Suggest something sensible, for heaven's sake.
GEORGE	Open a tin of sardines for the Vicar? A reverend might manage something with a loaf and a few small fishes.
MARY	Blasphemy will get you nowhere. (Tearful again.) And Emmeline Wagstaffe - I did want to show her that one didn't have to be a domestic science teacher to put on a tasty meal.
GEORGE	Here, look. We can still manage it. He's mown a path straight through the middle. Push the two ends together and who's to know? (He does so.)
MARY	Uncle Richard will, for a start. Whoever saw a fish that shape? It looks like a squat plaice. And there wouldn't be enough to go round.
GEORGE	Wait a minute. I take it that the tin-opener still functions?
MARY	Of course.
GEORGE	And that we have a tin of salmon in the house?
MARY	Don't be ridiculous. Tinned salmon's different. It isn't even the same colour.
GEORGE	And it's got a damned sight more taste. But we could fill the gap with it and cover up the patch with greenstuff - and you and I could eat that bit and give the genuine tasteless article to the guests.
MARY	But they'd see - (She rises, regarding the plate doubtfully.)
GEORGE	Not if you served it from the side table. Rather stylish that would be.
MARY	Uncle Richard is sure to -
GEORGE	Uncle Richard will be too busy telling how he caught the damned thing. I'll dash round with the Sauterne and distract attention. 'When in doubt, get 'em tight' is my motto.

MARY   I really can't think what else we –   (Looks at watch
                        in panic.)   Heavens! It's eight o'clock, and you
                        with no trousers on.

GEORGE   (climbing into trousers)   At least the cat hasn't got
                        them. Get on with repairing that fish while I cover my
                        nakedness.

MARY   (departing with the fish, wailing)   Why do such
                        things happen to me?

GEORGE   If you didn't make the cat the most important member
                        of the family, it might know its place. It's a damn
                        good thing that Uncle Richard gave us that salmon. If
                        we'd had to buy it, I'd have strangled the little beast
                        with my own hands.   (The bell rings, he struggles
                        into his jacket.)   That'll be the vicar and his
                        missus. Always the first to come and the last to go, on
                        the principle that light and heat are thus conserved in
                        the family home.   (Clutches his neck.)   Tie?
                        No tie!   (He finds it hanging round his neck.)
                        Tie.   (He ties it frantically as the bell rings again.
                        Coming. Coming.

MARY   (looking in)   George. Stop!

GEORGE   (skidding to a halt)   Eh?

MARY   (hoarse stage whisper)   Your zip.

                        (GEORGE looks blank.)

                        Do it up.

GEORGE   (doing so)   Lord! 'We have left undone those
                        things which we ought to have done up,' as the Vicar
                        almost said.   (He goes off and we hear his greeting
                        Hallo, Vicar. Hallo, Mrs Masters. Lovely to see you.
                        Let me take your coat, Mrs Masters. Do go in.

                        (Enter REVEREND and MRS MASTERS.)

VICAR   I do hope we aren't too early. You did say eight o'clo

GEORGE   (entering, adjusting tie)   Not a bit. In fact you're
                        all of two minutes late.

MRS MASTERS   (a rather vinegary woman)   I'm afraid we've
                        interrupted your dressing.

GEORGE   Not at all. Actually Mary didn't think you'd like the tie I had on, Mrs Masters, so I was changing it specially for you.

MRS MASTERS   How kind. It's a charming tie. One gets so tired of dog collars.

VICAR   My dear, they're a sign of my calling.

MRS MASTERS   But not becoming to the masculine neck, which in my opinion should be covered as much as possible. Mary! Can I help you?

GEORGE   (intercepting her passage to the kitchen)   No, no, Mrs Masters. There's nothing to do. Apart from the soup, it's a cold supper.   (Leads MRS MASTERS to a chair, R.)   As my wife said, 'After slaving at bun fights and parish teas,' she said, 'Mrs Masters deserves a break'.

MRS MASTERS   How kind.

GEORGE   I'll just tell her you're here and bring in the drinks. (He goes.)

VICAR   (disappointed)   Cold supper.

MRS MASTERS   I did hope it would be a good roast. That's why we had corned beef and salad for lunch.

VICAR   Mortification of the flesh is sometimes positively forced on one. Still –

GEORGE   (coming in with drinks)   Well, now. What are we going to drink? Mrs Masters? Gin, sherry – ?

MRS MASTERS   Thank you. Sherry for both of us. Dry. So kind.

GEORGE   (pouring out two, calling)   What are you having, darling?

MARY   (off)   Gin and tonic for me.

GEORGE   And me. Want any help?

MARY   (off)   Nearly finished. Could you take it in, dear, while I have a drink with the Reverend and Mrs Masters?

GEORGE   (going to kitchen)   Coming, love, coming.

VICAR   (ominously, after sipping sherry)   Cyprus.

MRS MASTERS   I knew as soon as I saw the decanter. People never use a decanter nowadays, unless they've something to hide.

VICAR   Not an altogether pleasing trait.

MRS MASTERS   Not very sensible, either. I put mine in a Bristol Cream bottle.

(Enter MARY.)

Oh, Mary, my dear, how nice to see you. I hope you haven't been working too hard.

MARY   Oh no. A very simple meal really.

VICAR   Still, even simple things can be complicated sometimes.

GEORGE   (swiftly crossing to the dining room with the plate held high so that the curious MRS MASTERS cannot see what's on it)   You're telling me.

MRS MASTERS   And how's your little cat? It's the brother of my little Rosie, you remember.

MARY   Well, yes – actually he's –

GEORGE   (re-entering)   Rosie's little brother is a damned great tom with no manners or morals. I've just booted him out of the house.

MRS MASTERS   Fancy. Our little Rosie has impeccable manners –

VICAR   (sadly)   But her morals leave much to be desired.

(A bell rings peremptorily.)

GEORGE   Ha! Guess who! Would you say that was a masculine or a feminine ring?

MRS MASTERS   Oh, definitely masculine. Very –

GEORGE   You don't know our Miss Wagstaffe, then. I've never seen anything more masculine than that woman.
(He goes.)

VICAR   Is that the domestic science mistress at the high school?

MARY   Yes. Emmeline Wagstaffe. She's got a heart of gold.

MRS MASTERS   And a voice like a foghorn. Yes, I know her.

GEORGE   (off)   Hullo, Emmeline, my old dear. How are you?

EMMELINE   Fighting fit, George, fighting fit and rearing to get at one of Mary's delicious meals.

(They enter.)

MARY   Oh, don't say that, Emmeline. I'm always at a disadvantage with you. You're an expert.

EMMELINE   Don't you believe it, my dear. There's a world of difference between showing little girls how to make fairy buns and being an expert, I can tell you.

MARY   You know the Vicar and Mrs Masters, don't you?

EMMELINE   I've only seen the Vicar from a worm's eye view below the pulpit. How d'ye do? Now that I see you on the flat, I realise how the pulpit gives you height. We all ought to have pulpits, to add to our stature if nothing else, ha! ha!

VICAR   I am sorry if you feel that I add nothing else.

EMMELINE   How are you, Mrs Masters? You came to the school's Open Day, didn't you? That was damn' good of you, considering what a faked-up swindle the whole thing is.

MRS MASTERS   (frigidly)   I am a governor of the school.

EMMELINE   Are you, by Jove? Then you'll know all about the faking. Gin, please, George.

(Bell rings.)

MARY   That'll be Uncle Richard. I'll go.   (Hisses as she passes GEORGE.)   Do something to break the ice, for goodness sake. The atmosphere's so frosty that I'm numb.   (She goes.)

GEORGE   (over-hearty)   Gin, Emmeline. Get your cockles warmed up.

EMMELINE   I would if I had the slightest idea where I keep them. Where do you keep your cockles, Vicar?

MRS MASTERS   Well, really!

VICAR   I - er - I always understood they were associated with the heart.

EMMELINE   I'm relieved. From the look on Mrs Master's face, I
                  thought they might be something embarrassing.

GEORGE   Well, let's warm 'em, whatever they are.

                  (They drink.   Enter MARY with UNCLE RICHARD, a
                  bluff, talkative old bore.)

MARY   Here's Uncle Richard. You all know Uncle Richard.

RICHARD   Everyone knows Uncle Richard. Richard Verdin for
                  verdant vegetables. Famed through the county. How
                  do, all.

EMMELINE   Those verdant vegetables you sent up to school on
                  Thursday were pretty pock-marked, weren't they? Even
                  a donkey wouldn't budge for those carrots.

RICHARD   Ah, bad time for carrots. Sherry, please, George.
                  You're brave, aren't you, Mary, asking an outspoken
                  Amazon like Miss Wagstaffe to a meal? If she doesn't
                  like it, she'll say so, you know.

EMMELINE   Nonsense! I've already told Mary that I'm quite
                  uncritical.

MARY   Well - I hope you'll turn a blind eye to any weak spots.

RICHARD   There won't be any. I've a special reason for knowing
                  that.

MARY   Yes. Actually it's Uncle Richard who has provided our
                  pièce de résistance tonight.

GEORGE   (aside, pouring sherry)   More of a pièce than he
                  thinks, I shouldn't wonder.

MARY   He caught the beautiful salmon we're having for supper.
                  Excuse me - I must just dish up the soup and take it in.
                  (She goes to kitchen.)

VICAR   (exchanging a significant glance with his wife)
                  Salmon. That does cheer me.

EMMELINE   And you caught it yourself? How splendid. I never
                  knew you were a fisherman, Mr Verdin.

RICHARD   (archly)   There's a lot about me you don't know,

	Miss Wagstaffe.
EMMELINE	I cast a very pretty fly myself. By Jove, Mr Verdin, this sheds quite a different light on you. I regard you with new eyes.
RICHARD	Why bother with new ones when the old ones are so fascinating?
EMMELINE	(uproariously coy) Oh, Mr Verdin –
RICHARD	Richard to you – Emmeline –
EMMELINE	Richard, then, you flatterer!
VICAR	A fascinating occupation, angling. So peaceful and relaxing.
EMMELINE	Peaceful? Relaxing? What do you mean?
VICAR	Have you not read your Isaak Walton? Every angler should. There is nothing to be compared with sitting on a bank beside a quiet river, communing with nature.
EMMELINE	Communing with my foot. We're talking about fly fishing. Real fishing. No sitting on a bank about that.
RICHARD	Standing on your feet, man, up to your thighs in icy water –
EMMELINE	Higher than that, sometimes.
RICHARD	(acting it) Casting again and again – watching, watching –
EMMELINE	(joining in) Waiting for the fly to be taken, striking at the crucial moment –
	(RICHARD strikes.)
RICHARD	(miming) Playing him – playing him – letting him do all the work –
EMMELINE	Slowly – gradually reeling him in –
	(RICHARD is reeling hard.)
RICHARD	(panting) Got the gaffe?
EMMELINE	(crouching forward) Ready – ? Ah! Got him. (She rises triumphantly.) Oh, well done, Mr Verdin.

MRS MASTERS   Is that how you caught tonight's supper?

RICHARD   Actually it was a bit more complicated than that.

GEORGE   For heaven's sake don't start him on a fishing story. He
                   never stops.

EMMELINE   Where did you catch him, Mr Verdin?

RICHARD   Sutter's pool. Just below the weir.

EMMELINE   Good place. Very good place.

RICHARD   Bad morning for the fly, though. Fish not rising at all.
                   I was just about to give up and go to the Jolly Anglers,
                   when suddenly - snap - and my reel was running out -
                   whizzing - nearly smoking with the speed.

EMMELINE   Oh, marvellous! Tally ho and all that.

RICHARD   I gave him enough rope to hang himself - if you'll
                   pardon the expression -

GEORGE   More sherry, Vicar?

VICAR   No, thank you.

GEORGE   Mrs Masters?

MRS MASTERS   No, really. No more.

RICHARD   And if he went up and down that stretch once -

GEORGE   Gin, Emmeline?

EMMELINE   (holding out her glass vaguely, intent on RICHARD)
                   Yes, yes?

RICHARD   He did it twenty times. And then he began to slacken -

GEORGE   More than Uncle Richard does when he starts a fishing
                   yarn.

RICHARD   And I began to reel him in. Oh, but he had a trick or
                   two up his gills, I can tell you.

EMMELINE   They always have. Fish are full of low cunning.

RICHARD   I was as wily as he was. I braced myself against a
                   tree -   (He braces himself against MRS MASTERS'
                   chair.)

EMMELINE	Yes, yes?
RICHARD	And slowly, steadily I began to reel him in, my rod bending almost double -
GEORGE	Go easy, Uncle. It isn't a barracuda, you know.
RICHARD	(deflated) No - well - anyway, I got him to the bank -
MARY	(entering with soup tureen) And there it is in the dining room. (She crosses to dining room, muttering to GEORGE as she goes.) For goodness sake stop him, George. He'll go on for ever.
GEORGE	You said break the ice. He's broken it.
RICHARD	Have I ever told you about the one I caught in Wales?
GEORGE	Yes, yes, a thousand times, yes!
EMMELINE	I don't think I -
MRS MASTERS	(hastily) How is your son Nigel, George? Is he doing well at University?
GEORGE	Hard to tell, really. He spent most of last term sitting down.
MRS MASTERS	Oh dear. Not an affliction of the nether limbs, I trust?
MARY	(re-entering from dining room) 'In,' George. Sitting in, not down. They're quite different.
GEORGE	Well, they've got to do the one to do the other, haven't they?
VICAR	(sadly) Sit-downs, sit-ins, love-ins - they're all the same, I fear. Just excuses to hide the fact that they are incapable of doing the work we are paying for them to do.
RICHARD	(nudging) You ever had a love-in with anyone, Miss Wagstaffe?
EMMELINE	(coyly) Is that a rude question or an invitation, Mr Verdin?
MARY	(defensively) I'm sure that Nigel was sitting in a good cause, whatever it was.

GEORGE   Sitting is about all he does do. He certainly doesn't
                communicate - not with me, anyway. He's got no
                vocabulary, that boy.

MARY   George! Only the other day you were complaining that
                he used words you never knew till you were twenty-five.

GEORGE   Oh, those words, yes. But ordinary conversation - he
                doesn't know what it is. He used ten times as many
                words at five years old than he does now. He fills in
                the gaps with 'I mean - ' 'You know - ' 'honestly - '
                and - oh yes - 'You're irrelevant'. That's the favourite,
                and it means us, my friends.

MARY   (briskly)   Well, at least he's learnt 'irrelevant'.
                He didn't use that at five. Anyway, the soup's in. So
                let's begin before it gets cold.

                (They all rise.)

                Uncle Richard, would you take in Miss Wagstaffe?

RICHARD   Will I not?

EMMELINE   Oh, good show. Your arm, sir. One almost feels one
                is in the Forsyte Saga.

RICHARD   Well, Emmeline, you may be an Irene, but I warn you,
                I'm no Soames.

EMMELINE   Glad to hear it. I like a warm man, myself.

GEORGE   (offering his arm)   Come on, Mrs Masters. Which
                Forsyte are you?

MRS MASTERS   Actually, I particularly dislike all the women.

MARY   Come along, Vicar. We mustn't let the soup get cold.

                (They go. The sound of chatter is heard for a few
                moments. Then a door off L. bangs and NIGEL and
                FELICITY enter. They are long haired and scruffy,
                clad in amorphous garments. FELICITY especially is
                hidden behind curtains of hair which she occasionally
                parts to peer through. She chews incessantly. They
                stop short as they hear laughter off.)

NIGEL   Oh God!

FELICITY   (morose)   Wha?

NIGEL   I forgot. They've got a party on.

FELICITY   Who?

NIGEL   The old folk.

FELICITY   (without enthusiasm)   Great. Let's join them.

NIGEL   What? Their party? You've gotta be joking, chick.

FELICITY   Why?

NIGEL   Well, I mean - old folks' parties. You know -

FELICITY   What?

NIGEL   They're grim. Honestly, you've no idea. They sit
             about on chairs. Round a table. They eat. Just sit
             and eat.

FELICITY   I wouldn't mind.

NIGEL   No music, stark, bright light, no atmosphere -

FELICITY   (aggrieved)   I'm hungry.

NIGEL   Static, man, static - you know -

FELICITY   You said there'd be food.

NIGEL   Oh Hell!

FELICITY   Bangers and chips would do.

NIGEL   Well, I'll see -   (He goes towards kitchen.)
             Girls!

FELICITY   (accusingly)   You said -

NIGEL   All right, all right. I said I'd see, didn't I?

             (Enter MARY with soup plates.)

MARY   (appalled)   Nigel! I thought you weren't coming
             in this evening.

NIGEL   Thanks for the welcome. I brought Felicity.

             (FELICITY glowers through her hair.)

MARY   (wanly)   Felicity too.   (She crosses with
             plates.)   Has the coffee-bar closed or something?

NIGEL   Yes. Police closed it.

MARY   (re-entering from kitchen)   Police? Nigel! Why?

NIGEL   Some clot left his cannabis on the counter.

MARY   Cannabis!

NIGEL   The fuzz found it. Silly half-wit. He must have been
                 pretty high to forget it. Anything in the fridge?

MARY   No. It's all on the table.

NIGEL   And that gutsy crowd will scoff the lot, I suppose.

MARY   (crossing to dining room)   The party is for them,
                 and you said you'd be out.

NIGEL   What about soup?

MARY   We've finished the soup. Your father's serving the
                 salmon now and I've no more time to waste.   (She
                 goes.)

NIGEL   Honestly -   How mean can you get?

FELICITY   You said -

NIGEL   (snapping)   I know I said. I forgot about the damn
                 party, that's all. Lend me 15p and I'll get some fish
                 and chips.

FELICITY   Haven't got 15p.

GEORGE   (coming in)   Look here, Nigel. You said you'd be
                 out.

NIGEL   Changed our minds.

GEORGE   (peering at FELICITY)   Who's that in there, then?

NIGEL   That's Felicity.

GEORGE   (regarding her gloomily)   Inappropriate in the
                 circumstances.

NIGEL   Lend me 30p, dad.

GEORGE   What for?

NIGEL   Fish and chips. We can eat them in the kitchen.

GEORGE   Oh no you don't. It'll smell.

NIGEL	Well, your fish smells.
GEORGE	It's a different sort of smell.
NIGEL	(aggressively) O.K. So yours is a high-class smell and ours is a low-class smell.
GEORGE	(equally aggressive) That's right.
NIGEL	Look, this is my home. I have a right –
GEORGE	It's your home and my house. And I have a right.
NIGEL	(to FELICITY) Come up to my room.
GEORGE	No!
NIGEL	Why not?
GEORGE	It's got a bed in it.
NIGEL	So's yours.
GEORGE	That's different. Besides, there's the vicar.
NIGEL	In my bed? God forbid.
GEORGE	Don't be daft.
MARY	(coming in) For heaven's sake! We can hear you. Go and finish your salmon, George. It's looking very pink. And talk. (GEORGE goes.) Look, stay here quietly and I'll bring anything that's left over. (She goes.)
NIGEL	Huh! The crumbs that fall from the rich man's table, as the vicar would say. Honestly – old folks – see why I want a flat?
FELICITY	Yeah.
NIGEL	(putting record on gramophone) There's no freedom nowadays. Whatever you do, they ask, 'Where are you going?' 'What are you doing?' 'Why are you late?' Makes a chap look a right berk.
FELICITY	Yeah.
	(Noisy pop music bursts forth. They jerk forlornly in time to it. After a few moments GEORGE appears with dish.)

GEORGE   (putting down dish and rushing to gramophone and
                lifting needle)   For pity's sake!

NIGEL   Oh, charming. Pardon us for existing.

GEORGE   That's more difficult than you'd think. We can't hear
                ourselves talk in there.

NIGEL   If Uncle Richard's doing the talking, we're doing you a
                favour. We thought we'd liven things up.

GEORGE   Look, we may not be able to compete with Felicity's
                vibrant personality, but we do have simple pleasures of
                our own.

NIGEL   Like Uncle Richard telling fishing yarns to that old
                lesbian, I suppose?

GEORGE   Now there you do her an injustice. She's hot-foot
                after Uncle Richard.

NIGEL   Ugh! Honestly - old people. You disgust me.

FELICITY   Yeah.

GEORGE   It's mutual. Here, eat up and get out.   (He
                proffers the dish.)

NIGEL   What's this, then?

GEORGE   Salmon.

NIGEL   Looks as if it's been bleached. Is it kosher?

GEORGE   Fresh salmon, you ignorant oaf.

NIGEL   Any booze?

GEORGE   (going)   No.

NIGEL   Just bloody-minded, parents are.

FELICITY   (scooping up fish with servers)   Yeah.

NIGEL   They bring you into the world and that's it, mate.
                We've had our chips.

FELICITY   (aggrieved)   I haven't. You said -

NIGEL   Oh, belt up. You've got something, haven't you?
                (He scoops up some.)   Tasteless muck.

FELICITY   Yeah.

NIGEL   Like wet cotton wool.

FELICITY   Yeah.   (But she eats on steadily.)

NIGEL   Tell you what -

FELICITY   Yeah?

NIGEL   Car's outside.

FELICITY   (perking up)   Yeah?

NIGEL   What you say we pick up Barney and go to the demo
             meeting? O.K.?

FELICITY   Yeah!   (She scrapes up a final spoonful and rises.)

GEORGE   (coming in)   Hallo. You off?

FELICITY   Yeah.

GEORGE   We shall miss you.   (He goes into kitchen.)

NIGEL   We're going to the demo meeting: something
             worthwhile.

GEORGE   Really?   (Returns with coffee cups which he sets
             on small table.)   What's a demo?

NIGEL   Demonstration.

GEORGE   And what are you demonstrating? Hedge-clippers or
             hair restorers?

NIGEL   We don't demonstrate anything. We demonstrate
             against. You know - protest marching.

GEORGE   You did that last week-end. Demanding a place in the
             Cabinet or something.

NIGEL   We do it every week-end.

GEORGE   (to himself)   Coffee cups - Percolator.   (He
             takes it from tray and turns to go out.)   What are
             you protesting about this time?

NIGEL   How the hell should I know? We're going to the
             meeting to find out.

GEORGE   (pausing and turning)   You mean to say you don't
             know?

NIGEL   Not yet. We protest. Every week. It's a way of life.
                Any objection?

GEORGE   (to FELICITY)   Do you protest?

FELICITY   Yeah.

GEORGE   Your eloquence must be invaluable to your cause.

NIGEL   Who are you to talk?

GEORGE   At least I can talk. I can say something more than
                'Harold out, Heath out, Enoch out'.

NIGEL   But what do you do? You just accept. You're
                irrelevant.

GEORGE   I knew it would come.

NIGEL   You don't protest about a thing.

GEORGE   (really roused at last, putting down percolator and
                advancing on NIGEL)   Look, son. I protested
                about Hitler all the way from Alexandria to Benghazi
                and from Normandy to Berlin. And I didn't have to be
                told what to protest about then, or now. And just at
                this moment, I'm protesting about you and your little
                poodle pal shlurping down salmon in the middle of our
                party and leaving hairs all over the furniture.

FELICITY   Charming.

GEORGE   We want this room and we want it now! Go and
                demonstrate somewhere else.

NIGEL   We were going anyway. Come on, Felicity.

                (They go.)

GEORGE   (sinking on to sofa)   God help England.

MARY   (entering)   George, what are you doing, sitting
                there talking to yourself? You came out to fetch the
                sweet from the fridge.   (Crosses to kitchen.)

GEORGE   Oh God! I thought I came to get the coffee.

MARY   (appearing with tray of dessert glasses)   You are the
                absolute end. We've been waiting and waiting –

GEORGE   Good for the digestion. At least I've got rid of the

cave man and his mate.   (He brushes the sofa.)
One of 'em's moulting.

(Sound of car.)

And he's taken the car!

MARY   Here, take these in and deal them out. We can't both
be out here at once. And talk. Keep the ball rolling.

GEORGE   What with keeping the ball rolling and dashing in and
out to deal with various crises, I've had mighty little to
eat this evening.   (Takes tray.)   What's this?
Idiot's Delight?

MARY   No, Angel's Breath.

GEORGE   I hope it's got that ring of confidence.

MARY   Get on. I'll leave you to eat in peace while I get the
coffee perking.   (She plumps up the cushions.)

GEORGE   (going)   I only hope Uncle Richard has finished the
story about the one he caught at Hay-on-Wye.
(Loudly and artificially as he goes.)   All right,
darling. If you're sure you can manage.   (Off.)
Mary's just seeing to the coffee.

MARY   (bitterly, as she goes to kitchen)   And you haven't
even got the milk off the doorstep.

(There is a burst of laughter from the dining room.)

VICAR   (off)   Angel's Breath, eh? Delightful.

(From the kitchen there is a piercing scream, a door
slamming, and MARY enters, milk bottle in hand.)

MARY   (in agonised whisper)   George! George!
(She casts an appalled glance back at kitchen. Then
assuming her 'company' voice she calls.)   I'm so
sorry, darling, but could you come for a moment?

GEORGE   (off, with artificial gaiety)   Coming, darling.
(Enters, talking back over his shoulder.)   You see,
she can't manage without her guide, philosopher and
friend - what the hell is it now?

MARY   (hysterically)   The cat, the cat!

GEORGE   Drunk all the bloody milk, I suppose. I'll kill the
                little perisher this time, I swear I will.   (He starts
                across.)

MARY   (wailing)   You won't.

GEORGE   You'll see if I won't.

MARY   He's dead already.

GEORGE   I'll tie a brick round his loathsome little -   (He
                registers.)   Dead?

MARY   (tearfully)   On the doorstep. Oh George! He
                must have crawled home to die when he felt the pains
                coming on.

GEORGE   Dammit, woman. He's a tom. How can he have pains
                coming on?

MARY   Poison. He's been p-p-poisoned.

GEORGE   What makes you think he's been poisoned, for God's
                sake?

MARY   What else could have killed him? He's lying there
                twenty yards from the road. He can't have been run
                over.

GEORGE   But who'd want to poison him? Besides me, I mean.

MARY   That's just it. We must have done it. He's only had
                that salmon to eat since breakfast.

GEORGE   Salmon? You think it was the salmon?

MARY   It must have been.

GEORGE   My God, - do you realise what you are saying?

MARY   Poor, poor little Tiddles.

GEORGE   Blast poor little Tiddles. What about them?

MARY   Who?

GEORGE   For crying out loud - the vicar and his missus, Uncle
                Richard and Emmeline. Do you want them expiring in
                galvanic jerks all over the dining room floor?

MARY   Tiddles means more to me than any of them.

GEORGE   But you can't be prosecuted for bumping off your own
                cat, whereas poisoning vicars and their mates is apt to
                raise awkward questions.

MARY   (realising)   Oh, George. Whatever shall we do?

GEORGE   We must tell them. Warn them of the possibility.

MARY   We can't, we can't.

GEORGE   We must.

MARY   It's too humiliating. It'll be all over the town.

GEORGE   If they curl up and die, it'll be all over the country.

MARY   Maybe it wasn't the salmon after all.

GEORGE   You were pretty sure a moment ago.

MARY   Well, I'm not now.

GEORGE   All the same, we've got to warn them - in case they
                feel ill. Then they can get treatment in good time. Is
                the milk on?

MARY   Not yet.

GEORGE   Go and put it on - fast. I'll deal with them. Lead up
                gently and then laugh it off. Go on. By the time the
                coffee's ready we'll all be having a good giggle over
                it.

MARY   (going)   Giggling? With Tiddles dead?

GEORGE   (at dining room door)   All right, folks. If you've
                finished eating and gossipping, p'raps you'll come in
                for coffee.

                (They enter, much more complacent.)

MRS MASTERS   Such a delicious meal. It's a long time since I had
                fresh salmon.

VICAR   My stipend doesn't run to these little luxuries.

GEORGE   Neither does ours. A good job we have a fisherman in
                the family.

RICHARD   Did I ever tell you about the one that got away in the
                Teme?

GEORGE   You did, Uncle Richard, you did. Sit here,
                Mrs Masters.

EMMELINE   Can't we wash up – or at least stack?

VICAR   Many hands make light work.

GEORGE   There's no room for many hands at the modern sink,
                Vicar.

EMMELINE   Well, if you're sure.   (She sits with a replete sigh.)
                You certainly did us proud with that salmon, Richard,
                old boy. A real beauty.

MRS MASTERS   With a first class fisherman and a first class cook, we
                couldn't very well go wrong, could we?

GEORGE   (sombrely to himself)   You'd be surprised.

VICAR   A most delicate flavour – there was something about it –
                a je ne sais quoi – that I couldn't quite place –

MRS MASTERS   There was, wasn't there? I noticed it, too.

GEORGE   (sotto)   Oh God!   (Aloud.)   So, you all
                feel fine, do you?

VICAR   'Juste bien' as the French say, – 'juste bien!' A most
                delightful wine, too.

GEORGE   No feeling of doubt? No internal uncertainty?

EMMELINE   Good gracious, no.

GEORGE   No little qualms?

EMMELINE   Qualms? Just the opposite. I feel fighting fit.

GEORGE   You too, Mrs Masters?

MRS MASTERS   Why, yes. I had an ample sufficiency, but I do nothing
                to excess.

GEORGE   Uncle Richard?

RICHARD   Expansive, my boy, expansive.

GEORGE   Oh good. I am relieved.

RICHARD   Why the inquisition? You been trying to poison us?

                (All laugh politely.)

GEORGE	Not trying to, Uncle, but something rather odd has occurred.
RICHARD	Odd? How odd?
GEORGE	(nervously) Not very - In fact, hardly at all. You'll die laughing when I tell you. At least - no, I don't mean that quite - I -
RICHARD	Out with it, George. What was odd? The soup or the sweet? There was certainly nothing odd about the salmon.
GEORGE	As a matter of fact, Uncle Richard, it may have been the salmon.
MRS MASTERS	(rising tremulously) What may have been?
GEORGE	The fact is, just before you arrived, the cat stole some of the salmon.
EMMELINE	Stole some? You mean it bit a chunk out of what we subsequently ate? How revolting.
GEORGE	(indignantly) It's a very clean cat - or was.
MRS MASTERS	(with a small shriek) Was? (She collapses into her chair.)
GEORGE	He's dead. We've just found him, stretched out on the doorstep. So we just wondered - as it was the last thing he ate - But as you all feel so jolly fit, there's nothing to worry about. I told Mary we'd all have a good laugh
EMMELINE	We all feel so jolly fit? I don't understand you. Why ask us at all? Why not go by your own feelings?
RICHARD	Precisely. Why worry us when you ate the stuff yourself?
GEORGE	Well - actually, we didn't.
VICAR	But I saw you.
MARY	(despairing, entering with percolator) We ate the tinned salmon that filled the gap the cat had left when it ate the middle.
RICHARD	Good God. It sounds like the house that Jack built.
VICAR	Tinned salmon.

MRS MASTERS   What deceit.

EMMELINE   I thought that salmon looked a damned funny shape.

RICHARD   It's outrageous. You poison us and get off scot free
                     yourself.

MARY   Nobody's poisoned you. You're all right. You said so.

RICHARD   My God, it's a plot. You're after my money.

MARY   Don't be ridiculous. You haven't any.

RICHARD   You've injected arsenic or something into it to bump me
                     off.

GEORGE   Rubbish. Just look at you. Bursting with health.

MARY   (brightly)   So it can't have been the salmon after
                     all. Coffee, anyone?

GEORGE   We mentioned it only out of a sense of duty – just in
                     case you felt off colour, so that you could take rapid
                     measures –

MRS MASTERS   (rising and clapping her hand to her mouth)
                     Bathroom – the bathroom.

MARY   (hastily ushering her out)   This way – quickly.

GEORGE   I hope she doesn't mean bathroom. They're separate.

VICAR   Good gracious – it's true then – poisoning.

GEORGE   Nothing of the sort. Pure auto suggestion. She's been
                     working up to it ever since I mentioned the cat.

VICAR   Are you implying that my wife is imagining that she is
                     feeling bilious?

GEORGE   Easily done – especially by the ladies.

RICHARD   (mopping his brow)   I'm no lady, but I'm feeling
                     decidedly off colour – sweating like a pig – shivery –

GEORGE   Nonsense. Here, have some coffee.   (He pours
                     some out.)

RICHARD   (taking it, it clatters in the saucer)   Look at that.
                     And you say I'm imagining it.

EMMELINE   (doubling up and clutching her stomach)   Ouch!

GEORGE — Oh Lord. Not you, too.

EMMELINE — Horrible gripes – sort of cramp – ah – ah! Ring for the ambulance –

GEORGE — Oh no, surely there's no need – not yet –

RICHARD — Not yet? What d'ye mean, not yet? Wait till we're dead, I suppose. I'll do it while I still have the strength.   (He lurches out U.L.)

VICAR — (palely, extracting his handkerchief)   I too feel far from – is there another bathroom?

GEORGE — No. But there's a loo in the hall if that's what you mean.

(The VICAR totters out.)

Door by the clock.

MARY — (coming in hurriedly)   Where's the sal volatile?

EMMELINE — (turning on her)   What the hell's the use of sal volatile when we all need stomach pumps?

MARY — All? Oh, no! Oh, George!

EMMELINE — Get the ambulance, you twittering fool.

MARY — Ambulance? Oh –

RICHARD — (re-entering)   I've rung already. Someone's got to do something.

EMMELINE — You say you tell us so that if we feel ill we can act quickly –

RICHARD — And when we are ill, you stand and gape.

GEORGE — You all felt fine till the moment I mentioned the cat –

EMMELINE — Oh, my poor guts. I feel as if I'd swallowed a cheese grater.

(Enter VICAR, handkerchief to mouth.)

MARY — Are you better,

VICAR — Only temporarily. It is not the end, I fear.

RICHARD — It damn soon will be if the ambulance doesn't arrive.

VICAR   Where did you say you caught that salmon?

RICHARD   Sutter's Pool.

VICAR   (accusingly)   Which is below the sewage works.

RICHARD   Five miles below. Effluent doesn't carry that far.

VICAR   (face crumpling)   Effluent! Ugh! Excuse me.
                        (He dashes out.)

EMMELINE   (turning on RICHARD)   How do you know it doesn't
                        carry? All rivers are polluted. The Duke of Edinburgh
                        says so. Oh Lord! It's ptomaine poisoning. Fatal.
                        (To RICHARD.)   It's all your fault. Catching
                        infected fish in filthy water. I'll sue you.

RICHARD   (enraged)   If you want the truth, I didn't catch the
                        fish in any bloody water, clean or filthy. So you can't
                        blame me, you old battle-axe!

GEORGE   What? Where did you get it then?

RICHARD   I bought it at Higgins's.

MARY   Why?

RICHARD   Because I was sick of you and George laughing at me
                        for catching nothing bigger than a perch. Grinning
                        behind my back. I knew.

MARY   So all those tales about the one that got away –

EMMELINE   And the one in the Teme –

GEORGE   And the one at Hay – ?

RICHARD   (banging sofa cushions)   Lies, lies, lies – and
                        you've got your revenge now, so don't look superior.

EMMELINE   So we don't know where the beastly fish came from.
                        (With sudden apprehension.)   Oh Lord! I hope
                        the bathroom's clear.   (She dashes out.)

RICHARD   (staggering out to hall)   Vicar! Open up there.
                        You've had one go already. Come out.   (He
                        disappears.)

                        (The ambulance bell is heard.)

GEORGE   Thank God. The ambulance.

MARY   (going to door of dining room to meet MRS MASTERS)
                        Help me, George.

                        (GEORGE goes to help support MRS MASTERS. Two
                        AMBULANCE MEN with a stretcher enter at the trot.)

MRS MASTERS   (faintly)   What will the Mothers' Union do without
                        me?

GEORGE   Disband, I expect. No more mothers.

FIRST
AMB. MAN   Where's the patient, then?

GEORGE   Here's the first. There are four.

SECOND
AMB. MAN   Four? What's been going on? A massacre?

                        (They pick up a squeaking MRS MASTERS, leaving her
                        suspended while they finish the conversation.)

GEORGE   Poisoning.

FIRST
AMB. MAN   Ah. An evenin' with Lucretia Borgia. Let's have you,
                        then.

                        (They lower MRS MASTERS on to stretcher and trot out.)

MARY   (wailing)   If only we'd eaten it too. It looks so
                        bad.

GEORGE   It would feel worse. Cheer up.

                        (Enter RICHARD and VICAR from hall.)

VICAR   Did I hear the ambulance?

GEORGE   You did. Your wife's already in it. Let me help you.

VICAR   Take your hands off me, sir. They have already caused
                        enough damage.

RICHARD   (with dignity)   The Vicar and I will support each
                        other – to the grave, if necessary.

                        (They go out L., as EMMELINE totters in R.)

MARY   Emmeline, my dear. How are you?

EMMELINE   If I don't have a prolapse after this it won't be your
                        fault.

           (The AMBULANCE MEN trot in again, seize her and bear her off.)

           The indignity - the humiliation - never have I been man-handled before -

FIRST   Cheer up, dear. At least you can say it's happened
AMB. MAN   once. Ready, Fred? Out over no man's land, then -

           (They go. MARY and GEORGE sink down exhausted. The ambulance bell is heard dying away. MARY suddenly springs to her feet.)

MARY   George. I've just realised -

GEORGE   Don't realise anything more.

MARY   Nigel and Felicity. They finished off the salmon. Oh, my poor boy! He must be lying in agony somewhere. Where did he go?

GEORGE   To some demo meeting.

MARY   Where?

GEORGE   God knows. Didn't say. Never does.

MARY   Well, do something. Get in the car and visit all his likely friends.

GEORGE   He seems to have taken the car. And all his friends are most unlikely.

MARY   I hope they'll realise it's serious when he starts being ill.

GEORGE   They'll just think he's taken a trip.

MARY   (stamping)   George! He's your son. He must be got to hospital - at once. Ring the police.

           (A door bangs. NIGEL comes in from kitchen.)

           Oh Nigel, my darling boy - you're safe. How are you feeling?

NIGEL   Lousy. Why?

MARY   George. Phone for the ambulance again. Where's Felicity?

NIGEL	Finished.
MARY	Already? Oh, surely not?
NIGEL	I mean, I've finished with her. I've chucked her.
GEORGE	Why?
NIGEL	She talked too much. (He sits, sulkily.)
GEORGE	You're going to be hard to please, aren't you? What about the meeting?
NIGEL	Off. No-one turned up.
GEORGE	A demo against demos perhaps.
MARY	(enraged) George! Your own son is in deadly peril and you stand there gassing about demos. I'll get the ambulance, if you won't.
NIGEL	What the hell are you on about? There's an ambulance just gone up the street if you want one.
MARY	We don't. You do.
NIGEL	You need a padded cell. You must be bonkers. Why should I need an ambulance, for heaven's sake?
GEORGE	Look. You ate that salmon, didn't you?
NIGEL	Correct. It tasted like boiled dish cloths. Why?
GEORGE	Because you ought to be writhing in agony.
NIGEL	Well, I'm not. I'm just fed up. First the cat, and then Felicity.
	(Pause.)
GEORGE	What do you mean – 'First the cat'?
NIGEL	(surprised) Didn't you read the note I left underneath him?
MARY	(faintly) What note?
NIGEL	It was his fault – honestly. I didn't know he was under the car. I'm sorry, mum.
GEORGE	(shaking him) What are you saying? What did you do to that cat?

NIGEL   Well, I started off the car pretty sharpish and ker-blonk there he was behind the back wheel. He can't have felt a thing.

MARY   You mean - ?

GEORGE   So it wasn't - ?

NIGEL   I didn't want to spoil the party, so I left him on the doorstep with a note - explaining.

GEORGE   Mary! We're in the clear. Our honour is unstained. (He begins to laugh.)

MARY   Stop it, George, stop it. It's worse than ever it was.

GEORGE   To think of that lot, stretched out in hospital, with the stomach pumps sluicing away -

NIGEL   Will anyone kindly tell me - ?

MARY   Shut up! George! Will you stop laughing like a maniac. They'll be doing dreadful things to them. Ring the hospital.

GEORGE   Not I. They asked for it. Nasty, ungrateful, mean-minded little -

MARY   Nigel. You ring the hospital. I'm in no state to explain.

NIGEL   Neither am I. I haven't the faintest idea what you're on about. What do I tell them?

GEORGE   To stop pumping.

NIGEL   Pumping what?

GEORGE   Sewage.

NIGEL   In a hospital? If only you'd explain.

MARY   (wailing)   They'll never forgive us - never.

GEORGE   Who cares? Let them stew in their own revolting juices.

NIGEL   (shouting)   For Pete's sake - what's happened?

GEORGE   (pouring out drinks for himself and NIGEL, mock solemn)   Nigel, my boy, you have done a far far better thing this day than you have ever done.

NIGEL   (incredulously)   I have?

GEORGE   (handing him drink)   You have at one fell swoop
rid us of Tiddles and four friends who are unworthy of
the name. My boy, I give you a toast. 'All hands to
the pumps.'   (He drinks.)

(MARY bursts into loud hysterical wailing and NIGEL
stands agape.)

CURTAIN